Balou

By Brian Borgford

Thanks to all my readers of Pepper who motivated me to write the story of Balou.

Chapter 1

Humane Sunrise

Her large white paws clomped across the newsprint covering the concrete floor, slipping whenever they came in contact with some of her own feces scattered around the wire mesh cage. She flopped on her belly, crunched up some paper with her front paws and began to gnaw on it. Not as tasty as the liquid nourishment her mother provided only days earlier. And certainly not as cozy as when she had six siblings crowded around her. Her short puppy memory was fading with each rising sun, which barely poked through the cracks in the ceiling, providing scant warmth for the prison she now occupied. She flopped her head on her paws, closed her eyes and dreamed.

She jumped when she heard the clank of the gate to her cage and recoiled from the large hand that reached for her head. With no place to run in the tiny confines of her prison, she succumbed to the touch of the hand on her head – a light pat, then a scratch behind the ears. It felt good and she snuggled close to the arm that provided the compassion she had not experienced since what seemed like the long-ago days of her mother's lolling tongue. In an instant it was over and a pan of water with some crunchy food remained instead. She lapped every morsel, satiating her aching belly. Then again she slept.

Yelping and barking coming from all directions were both frightening and comforting as she awoke with a start. The sounds were those of other helpless and lonely animals, but it gave proof to the white pup that she was not alone in her prison. She had no way of discerning day from night, nor the ability to count the number of rising suns that had passed since she first opened her eyes in this lonely cage.

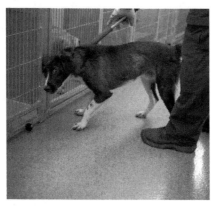

Some of her companions were already trapped in adjoining cages when she arrived. Each day, one of the humans retrieved a different one of her neighbours, in loving arms, accompanied with the words she could not understand, "Sorry boy. Your turn today." The neighbour never returned and was replaced with a different canine.

Each day she awaited the loving attention and nourishment that came from the humans that made the rounds. The soft words meant nothing, but they sounded so soothing to her tender ears, "Last supper Whitey. Tomorrow's your day. I'm gonna miss you." Again she slept with a full belly and the memory of a soft hand on her head, oblivious to the horrid fate that was planned for her the next day.

She awoke to a different set of steps

clanking towards her cage. She awaited her usual meal, drink and attention, but a different face appeared at the front of the cage. He had a broad smile and as much hair on his lip as he had on his head. "This is the one, for sure. I'll take him."

"It's a her. And you arrived just in time. Today was to be her last day," responded the familiar attendant. "Before you adopt, you need to pay for spaying. We can't let a dog out of here that is going to reproduce more of her kind. Pay at the cashier and you can pick her up tomorrow after the operation."

The words were just noises and didn't contain the soft reassurances of the previous sounds coming from the mouths of the humans. With a gentle hand, her familiar human lifted her from the cage and held her tight to his breast. This was heaven.

"You wanna hold her for a bit before I take her?"

"Sure," said the newcomer, as he lifted the pup to his shoulder. It wasn't quite as comforting as her human, but the attention still felt good as she lay her head on his shoulder, not wanting to be set down.

Back in the arms of her attendant, she started to shiver as he walked her down a long unfamiliar hallway to a room with a metal table. He set her on the table, which was too slippery for her to stand, so she flopped on her tummy, as a man in a white coat approached with a menacing sharp stick in his hand. She quivered and yelped as the tool pierced her skin with pain she had never experienced. She tried to nip at the hand of the white-coated man, but before she could reach, she fell on the table in a stupor.

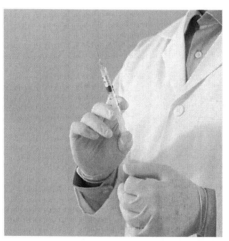

When she awoke, she recalled the pain of the stick to her skin, but that memory faded with the realization that her belly was full of other sharp pains. She yelped and whimpered.

"Change that dressing a couple times for the first few days and she'll be fine," said the man in the white coat who was speaking to the hairy man who had held her outside her cage the prior day.

"I'm going to call you Balou," said the man who was about to become her master. His voice was clumsy, but caring, and Balou felt reassured as he lifted her, taking care not to touch the area with the stiches. The man carried her into the daylight, causing her eyes to squint, never having been outside in the fresh air. She cringed at the vast expanse of the big sky, but her tail wagged at the unfamiliar sense of freedom.

Chapter 2

A New Sunrise

As Balou snuggled closer to her new master while lying on a soft bench of the machine that moved, her eyes drooped and she began to doze with the rhythm of the conveyance causing a pleasant humming in her ears. She was getting used to the constant stream of words emanating from the mouth of her master, who seemed to be directing these comforting words at her. Just as her eyes fell shut, she was jerked awake by a flash of light in her eyes and a putrid odour in her nose. The man had taken a white cylinder from a box in his pocket, placed it between his lips and the rasped a small stick against a paper in his hand when the explosion occurred and a flame was pushed into her face. She yelped in fear, and then in pain from her sore belly, as she pushed herself away from the source of the light towards the door of the vehicle.

"It's OK girl. Settle down. It's just a match. Look, here's another one," the man said trying to sooth the terrified puppy but in doing so flashed another freshly lit match into her face, bringing her to full panic as she tried to escape her moving prison. "You'll get used to it," he continued as he inhaled some blue air into his mouth and then blew it into Balou's eyes. She backed even closer to the door, shaking and now sneezing, placing her paws over her eyes and snout as she whimpered. She didn't come near the man for the rest of the ride in the vehicle.

When the vehicle came to a stop, Balou froze, not knowing what would happen next. The man opened the door, again uttering some calming sounds from his mouth and then eased the puppy into his arms trying to avoid touching the tender parts from the operation, and carried Balou into her new home.

"Hey guys. Look what I have. She's our new roommate. Meet Balou. Balou meet your new roommates, this is Robert and this is Dave. Oh and I'm Don; I'm your new master."

"Balou? Where'd you get that name from?" shouted Robert. "Isn't that the bear in the Jungle Book?"

"That's Baloo – B-A-L-O-O. This is Balou – B-A-L-O-U – as in Cat Balou. You know, Jane Fonda?" Don explained.

"She's shaking," Dave commented. "I

thought you were getting a real dog, not a little coward."

"She's only a pup and just had her innards worked on. Thy guy at the Humane Society said he thought she was a white German Shepard and will grow pretty big. Look at the size of her paws."

Don set the puppy on the floor, "Go – check out your new home." But Balou just sat with a puzzled and fearful look on her face. She was still shivering and sore.

"Guess she won't be much of a guard dog," Robert said.

"She'll get used to the place. Hey watch this," Don said as he reached for his matches. Balou's eyes went wide. Don scratched the match across the cover causing another minor explosion that he pushed at Balou's face. She yelped and limped under the nearest piece of furniture to hide from the light and hideous smell. The three young men all roared with laughter at the puppy's reaction to the match.

"That's OK girl. Come on out," Don said as he crawled on his hands and knees to retrieve Balou from her hiding place. "You're gonna see lots of matches here. We all smoke, so get used to it. We'll just keep at it and she'll get used to it. If we keep flashing the matches in her face and blowing smoke at her she'll get to like it. That's what they do with hunting dogs, just keep firing off the gun until they're used to it."

Don set out a plate of dog food and a pan of water. Balou edged up to the dishes to test out what had been presented, but she kept a wary eye for any other perils that may haunt her new home. She jumped at every noise and every movement of the three boys watching for the next time she would face the hot flare in her eyes.

In spite of the terrors she had faced in her first day in her new home, she had the most comfortable sleep since she was separated from her birth family. Don took her into his bed and cradled her in his arms as Balou fell into a deep sleep, twitching her body and legs with the dreams that came from such a state. The night passed too quickly as she awoke to the sulfur smell in her face as

Don lit up his first smoke of the day. Balou sprinted off the bed and buried herself far underneath to escape the blinding flash and awful smell. Don reached under the bed to drag her out for her next lesson.

A new adventure arose, as Don took Balou for her first walk outside. She was still too small, with her short legs, to manipulate the stairs leading to the house, so Don had to carry her to the sidewalk. The outdoors was filled with wonder as she sniffed the ground, picked at the grass and pawed insects as they crossed her path. Upon returning from the first walk, Don encouraged Balou to try the stairs on her own, but she could only raise her paw at the tall barricade and whimper for help. Once inside, she glanced at the long staircase leading to a dark place at the top. "You can't go up there, girl. Our neighbours wouldn't like it if you started bugging them. You just stay on our level," Don said with his gruff, but soothing voice.

The three boys disappeared during the days, leaving Balou alone in Don's bedroom.

She occupied herself by finding loose socks and clothing and gnawing at them with her needle like teeth. Upon returning, Don chastised Balou and slapped her backside when he saw the chaos around his room. This gave Balou one more reason to run and hide under whatever piece of furniture she could find.

Balou's days soon settled into a predictable routine. She ran and hid every time the cigarette package came out, she went for walks with Don in the mornings and evenings, she sat alone in the room while they boys vanished for the better part of the day. She was well fed and comfortable and when she wasn't alone, Balou was always the centre of attention with the boys and their friends.

As she grew bigger, Balou was able to navigate the front steps on her own on their travels in and out of the house; but when she tried to climb the long staircase at the front entrance Don always gave her a swat and shout, "No."

Balou had established a series of places to hide whenever the boys flashed the matches in her face, but with her increasing size she had more difficulty squeezing into some of the spaces. It was more difficult to escape the terror and torture these otherwise good natured young men inflicted on her. She loved the attention they bestowed on her, but was always kept a wary eye for the instruments of terror that brought her happy times to an end.

Chapter 3

The Light from Above

At the flash of the match, Balou tried to escape under the sofa, but could no longer squeeze in the small space, so she panicked and jumped over one set of outstretched legs and into the front hallway. When she saw the forbidden staircase, she scampered up as fast as her growing legs would carry her and cowered at one of the doors, her tail twitching with fear causing a knocking sound on the door. The door opened and a new man stood there looking down at the shivering half-grown dog. "Well hello. What's your name?" he questioned the unresponsive animal. With the door now open Balou scooted past the man's legs and into the new room that presented more hiding places from her terror.

"Hello, anyone home," Don shouted up the stairs.

"Yeah, we're here Don. C'mon up. Looks like we have something of yours up here."

"I'm so sorry Brian," Don said as he entered the room looking for his escaped pet. "I won't let that happen anymore. Balou, that's her name, just got scared with all the people over."

"No problem," Brian responded. His wife, Marlene, was sitting on the sofa petting the now soothed animal. "She's welcome here anytime," Brian continued.

This was the first of many sprints up the stairs that Balou would make as a means of escaping her tormentors. The good times she experienced with Don, his roommates and their friends always ended with the terror of the flash in her face. The upstairs people, who had the same instruments of terror that the boys possessed, did not inflict the same fear with their tools.

Much of Balou's free time was now spent sprinting up the stairs whenever the couple was home, and even when they weren't. They often returned to their upstairs home to find Balou lying beside the door to their apartment. Sometimes they returned

Balou to Don, but often Don had to come up the stairs to retrieve his pet.

Chapter 4

Another Sunrise

"We're moving, Don," Brian mentioned on one of Don's foray's to retrieve Balou. "Marlene and I have bought a house. We're thinking of starting a family."

"That's too bad. Oh, not about the family, but that you're moving," Don replied. "We're really going to miss having you guys around. You're great neighbours, especially to put up with a bunch of partiers like us."

"We get to take advantage of your parties, so we're going to miss it here too."

"I think Balou is going to miss you the most," Don said as he looked down at his almost full grown dog.

"Yeah, we're gonna really miss her too. We've grown pretty attached to her."

Moving day saw little need for more than a half-ton truck from the farm and Brian's 1963 Valiant, as the furnished apartment only a contained a few boxes of personal possessions. Balou cocked her head at the strange movements of all the people up and down the stairs, carrying boxes to the waiting vehicles.

"Good luck with your new home," Don said as he shook hands with Brian and gave Marlene a hug. "Make sure you invite us to the housewarming."

"We sure will," Brian replied. "It should be before the end of the month. Make sure you bring Balou."

"That's what I wanted to talk to you about," Don said as he pulled two bags from the front porch. One contained the few toys that he had accumulated for Balou and the other was a large bag of dog food. "I think Balou is better off with you guys in your new house. She's always at your place anyway." His hand brushed up to his eye and he turned away from Brian.

Brian hesitated and glanced at Marlene who gave a shrug of resignation and a reluctant nod. "Are you sure about this? She's your dog."

"I've thought long and hard and I'm sure. She tolerates us, but she loves you guys. Besides we can always come and visit when we need a Balou fix."

"OK, we'll do it," Brian formed a broad grin as he shook Don's hand. He opened the door to the car and Balou jumped in without so much as a backward glance.

Chapter 5

Endless Sunshine

Life in her new home was paradise for Balou. She was allowed to go outdoors on her own, but was fearful of straying too far. Daily, Brian took her for long walks in the nearby fields where she could chase birds into the air and follow gophers to their holes where she dug after them with no hope of ever catching one.

Although there were many homes like theirs nearby, there was no grass, roads or sidewalks. Everyplace was dirt and mud, as the new development had yet to complete the roads and walkways. Balou was always covered in dirt and mud when she returned the house. Brian forced her to lie on her back while he cleaned her feet and belly before she could enter the rest of the house. This became an automatic ritual for Balou as she rolled on her back after every trek outside to await the comforting cleaning process.

At night she lay between Brian and Marlene in the big bed, pushing each of them to the outer edges, as her increasing bulk required more and more space.

There was a constant supply of water, and food twice each day and a steady stream of treats. She learned that if she did little tricks, like standing on her hind legs, or rolling over, she could coerce biscuits from the couple at will.

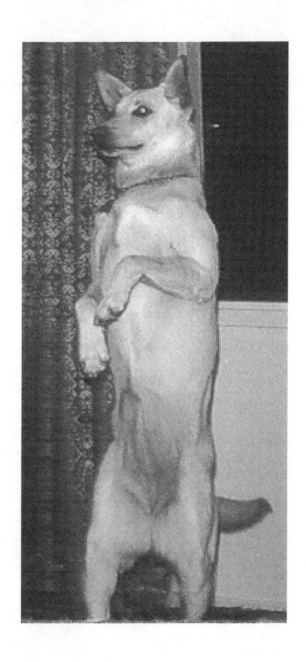

Her saddest times were when she was relegated to the concrete room at the bottom of the entry way. This happened most days of the week, early in the morning, and she had to stay there until her masters returned from wherever they went all day. She was free to rejoin the couple in the comfort of the upstairs once they returned at the end of each day.

It wasn't an uncomfortable time, with a soft couch to lie on, but it was lonely. Balou loved her masters and hated when she couldn't be with them. If only she could spend these lonely days in the familiar surroundings of the upstairs living area.

Chapter 6

Escape to the Sunshine

On one of her lonely days trudging around the basement, Balou wandered to the door leading to the upstairs. She pushed at the edge of the door with her nose and it wiggled, so she pushed some more and it wiggled again. She placed her paw on the door and it moved even more, so she jumped up on her hind legs and pushed the door with the whole weight of her now large body and the door sprung open. She eased down on her four legs and watched the door swing to a fully open position, bump against the wall and creep to a closed position again. This time it only took a gentle nudge from her paw or a push from her snout to repeat the process. She amused herself with the play action of opening the door and watching it close several times before deciding to walk through the door to the stairs leading to the living area she was familiar with. She sensed that she wasn't supposed to be up here in the absence of her masters so she took slow steps and kept her head low while pushing her ears low on her head.

She spent most of the day wandering through the living area, chewing on a sock she found on the floor, pulling a few papers out of the trash, standing on her hind legs with her front paws on the window sill watching the outdoors. It was then that she spied the car with her owners driving towards the house. Balou panicked. She knew she wasn't supposed to be here and she didn't want to disappoint her kindly masters. She rushed towards the basement and found the door closed. But there was enough of a crack that when she used her snout and her paw, she was able to ease the door open and rush to lay on the sofa, with the door closing behind her.

"Hey Balou, we're home," called Brian as he burst down to retrieve the dog lounging comfortably on the sofa, wagging her tail at his entrance. She rushed up to him and erected herself on her hind legs letting her front paws land on Brian's chest as he caressed her ears and let loose with a stream of soft words.

"Brian, is the dog down there?" Marlene shouted from upstairs.

"Yeah, we're coming up," Brian replied.

"She's been up here," Marlene scolded

as she looked at Brian.

"Don't be silly, she was lying on the sofa and the door was closed."

"Look at this sock, and these papers. That's Balou's work."

"Balou, were you up here?" Brian said to Balou is his disciplinary voice.

Balou's ears went down and she lowered her head in obvious guilt.

"That must have been from before. There is no way she can get out of the basement," Brian assured Marlene.

The next day Brian again went to the basement to retrieve Balou and again Marlene complained that there was evidence of Balou's presence. Brian assured Marlene that Balou could not get through the closed door, but Balou's guilty look raised Brian's suspicions.

The third day Marlene shouted in hysterics, "Where is my chicken? I left a whole cooked chicken on the counter to make chicken salad and there's nothing left but a clean plate, no bones or anything. That dog is getting up here; I know it."

The following day the couple left as they did every morning, but this time Brian slipped out of the started car and slinked to the front door listening for any sound from inside. A faint clunk indicated there was some movement inside and when he opened the door he spied Balou creeping up the steps from the basement. When she saw Brian, Balou lowered her ears and crouched in fear of the retribution of the penalty she might face for her deviant behaviour. Brian gave her a light tap on her backside followed by the words, "bad dog," which Balou understood mean she was not doing what she was supposed to be doing.

Brian brought Marlene back into the house to display the findings of his detective work. "Look, the door seems to be latched, but if you don't pull it hard enough it doesn't click all the way. Balou has learned how to push the door until it flops open, then the door just falls closed on its own, but still ajar so that Balou can nose her way back in," he explained. "See, now if I push it hard, the latch goes in all the way and there is no chance of her shoving it open. I'll just have to make sure I secure it tight each time."

The next week brought no more evidence of Balou's escape from her daytime home. Brian and Marlene congratulated themselves at solving the problem and spent no more time worrying about Balou making a mess upstairs.

Every day, Balou tried to push with her snout and push with her front paws, but the door remained shut. She persevered, wanting so badly to be in her favourite upstairs territory, but with no success. Then she started playing with the door knob that she knew her masters used to control the opening of the door. She placed her paws on the knob to make it move from side to side. She had little else to spend her boring days on, so she kept pawing the door daily. After several days of working on the door knob, her paws moved the knob in a full rotation and the door sprung open; she was again free to roam the living quarters. She always examined the contents of the garbage can. It often contained treasures that could be consumed. Chewing on a sock or a shoe caused a soothing sensation on her teeth and gums. She crawled into the bed to have a nap in her usual place, even though it was not as comforting without the couple on each side. Then when the day was over and she heard the car coming down the residential road, she returned to the basement to await her release and claim her rightful attention for being abandoned each day.

"She's at it again," Marlene screamed at Brian. "Balou has been upstairs." Brian tried to protest in Balou's defense but the evidence of her presence was overwhelming, even though her method of escape was a mystery.

Brian again set about his detective work to see if he could catch Balou in the act. He pretended to exit the house, but just stood at the front door to await Balou's next steps. He didn't have to wait long before his heard the scratching at the basement door, saw the door knob turn and the door fling open under Balou's weight. Balou crouched with her ears bent down when she saw Brian at the top of the stairs. Her physical punishment was mild, but the angry tone of his master's voice hurt more than any slap on the rump. Her crime was not in doing, but in being caught.

Balou never made her way through the basement door again as no amount of clawing or pressure would move the barricades that had been placed in front of the door to prevent her escape. The upstairs was now beyond her reach, but escaping was part of her nature and she never ceased to look for ways out of this prison.

Chapter 7

Outdoor Sunshine

"Look, Balou is sitting on our front step," Marlene exclaimed as they drove up to the house.

"Balou, how did you get out here?" Brian questioned the unanswering dog who jumped up on the couple to claim her end of the day attention. "I'll bet the meter reader must have let her out by accident."

Balou had perfected a new escape. The sofa, where she rested, sat right next to a big desk. If she got on top of the desk, she could stretch her long body far enough to reach the sliding basement window. With considerable effort and a few harmless tumbles she was able to slide the unlatched window, which was left slightly open for ventilation, to the side and push her claws in to the mesh screen pulling it open just far enough that she could grab the window sill with her front paws and push at the concrete wall with her back paws until she squeezed through the narrow opening she had created. She never wandered from her yard as she dug holes in the dirt and basked in the sunlight on the front step. These outside days were far better than lying on the sofa in the dark basement.

"I got a call from Judy today saying

that she saw Balou crawl out our basement window. I thought she was nuts, but obviously she was right," Marlene said after seeing Balou outside a second day.

The next day the sofa and the desk were relocated to a windowless wall and Balou had lost her last means of escape and resigned herself to waiting in the basement until her masters returned each day.

Chapter 8

Trapping the Sunshine

The first spring in the new house created a muddy mess on the unfinished streets and yards. Balou had to endure being lugged by Brian from the car, which had to be parked a long way from the house, to avoid being stuck in the mire. This routine lasted until sidewalks and roads began to appear. Soon the outdoors was full of people engaged in activities in their yards. The world outside was changing before Balou's eyes, as new structures were appearing every day.

Balou loved the weekends when Brian and Marlene were home all day and spent their days working in the yard. Balou could roam freely, dig in the dirt, chase birds and try to catch the little whistling rodents that ran into holes in the ground whenever Balou got too close.

The wide open space in the neighbourhood began to take on closed in appearance as all the home owners began to erect wooden barriers between the yards. Brian and his father, along with a yappy runt of a dog named Snooky, began erecting a wooden barrier around their own home. This didn't appear to be a happy time, as there seemed to be constant anger and shouting as the pieces of wood never seemed to respond to the orders they were given by the men.

During these times, Balou tried to make friends with Snooky, a four-pound poodle, but the runt rarely let Balou near her, snarling and snapping if Balou came too close while Snooky stayed near the old man who was her master. When Snooky did run loose, Balou tried to chase her, but she yelped, snapped and hopped on to the lap of her owner, the old man who just seemed to sit on a chair talking while Brian and his neighbour fought with the pieces of wood.

The appearance of the yard took on a new look after the struggles of the men produced a barrier around the circuit of the back yard.

"Now we can keep Balou from wandering," Brian said to his neighbour as they hung the final piece of wood, the gate. "Let's lock her in the back yard and we can go sit on the front step for a beer and see how she handles her new enclosure."

Balou liked being outdoors but never liked being alone and couldn't understand why the two men abandoned her behind this wooden prison. She could hear the men talking and laughing in the distance and wanted to be with people, not by herself in the yard. She jumped up on the newly erected fence and felt it vibrate and clink as she threw her paws against the gate. A couple more attempts and she realized that if she threw her paw against the metal latch, the gate swung open and she could join the people in the front yard.

"Balou, how did you get out?" Brian scolded. He and the neighbour walked Balou back to the open gate. "I guess I never closed it properly. In you go," Brian instructed Balou, who obeyed and walked back into the yard while Brian snapped the gate shut and secured the latch. Alone again, Balou repeated her previously learned skill and hit the latch with her front paws. The gate swung open and she joined the two men in the front yard.

"What the….," Brian began, "How did you…," Brian put Balou back behind the gate, but this time he stayed and watched her. He called her to come as he stood on the other side of the gate. Balou was only too happy to show her skill at opening the gate. Brian's shoulders slumped at another defeat perpetuated by his innovative dog. He solved the problem by putting a wire "lock" on the latch to prevent it from flying loose as Balou's paws flailed at the unmoving latch.

"Got 'er figured out now. Problem solved," Brian brushed his hands and smiled at his successful maneuver. "Now the back yard is your home," he said directly to Balou.

During the days of spring and summer, Balou was free from the confines of the dingy basement and had the large back yard in which to roam and play while her masters were away. But Balou was never content to be confined to one area. She wandered and sniffed the length of the fence and found that if she pawed at the ground at the bottom of the boards, the dirt easily moved, creating a space large enough for her to squeeze under the fence. She then weaved her way to the front yard and lay basking on the sunlit front step waiting for her masters to arrive. She ran up to the car to greet them on their return, but she wasn't greeted as warmly in return.

"What are you doing out?" Brian admonished the now sullen canine, with her ears down and her head lowered. Brian walked to the gate, finding it secure and scratched his head as he scanned the yard for evidence of her method of escape. Several days of this mystery passed before Brian walked the entire yard looking for clues before finding the hole under the fence. He filled it in with some concrete blocks and cut off this escape route.

Balou's appearance in the front yard on subsequent days forced Brian to fill in several new holes that kept appearing until most of the fence had a foundation of concrete blocks preventing further digging. Finally Balou had no more routes of escape and she contented herself with waiting in the back yard until her daily release.

Chapter 9

Sunshine the Cat

Balou wandered the fence from end to end looking for a way out, but none was to be found. She knew from experience that there were wonders beyond her own yard, but she had to be content to view them through the slats of the fence.

Balou spied a four-legged creature

wandering in the next yard and she yipped with excitement at the animal. The animal stopped and looked in Balou's direction, hearing her beckoning, but a quick glance confirmed its indifference to the noise and it kept ambling along its chosen route.

"Sunshine, where are you," a woman shouted from the door of a nearby house. The animal stopped and listened to the sound of the woman's voice, but then ignored it and kept moving without any apparent urgency. "There you are, you bad kitty," the woman shouted as she ran from her house in pursuit of the animal. The cat, apparently named Sunshine, looked back at the woman in obvious disgust and stood waiting for its inevitable capture. The woman scooped up the cat in her arms and began hugging and kissing the disinterested cat. "You are a bad kitty, running off like that," the woman cooed as she disappeared back into her house with the cat still in her arms.

Balou just stood and watched, while uttering a few anxious whimpers, wanting to know more about this enigmatic creature. Balou watched this scene repeat several times. Each time the cat showed more interest in Balou's existence before being spirited back into its house by the woman. Each time, the cat came closer and closer to Balou's yard before being captured.

One day the cat bounded to the top of the fence and looked down upon Balou as she stood on her hind legs to get a better look. All the while she was whining with excitement over this potential new friend. She tried to jump up to greet the elusive cat, but could never reach the top of the fence. The cat watched Balou's futile attempts and hissed in response.

Sunshine began to make a daily routine of teasing the big white dog from her perch atop the fence. He sat and meowed at Balou who whined and jumped trying to reach the cat who feigned disinterest. One day Sunshine, showing no fear, jumped from her perch on the fence top and landed on the ground several feet from Balou. Balou saw this as a chance to complete the friendship and bounded over to the cat. Sunshine arched his back, raised his tail and let out a loud hiss, while bearing his teeth at Balou. Balou stopped short of reaching the cat, her ears lowered, and she crouched to the ground to show she meant no harm. Sunshine let out another loud hiss and darted across the yard and pounced up on the fence with Balou in pursuit. Balou again whined and jumped at the cat sitting atop the fence.

Sunshine took delight in performing this act daily upon the frustrated dog before the woman found him and spirited back inside the house. Balou could not find a way to tame the agile feline.

The next time Sunshine antagonized Balou, she ran as close to the cat as she could, repeating the daily routine, but as the cat hissed at the canine, Balou dropped to the ground and rolled on her back to demonstrate her intent to do no harm. Sunshine responded by converting her hiss to a mild meow. He wandered closer to the shivering dog and touched his nose to Balou's. Balou shot out her tongue with a friendly lap across Sunshine's face. Sunshine swiped his paw across Balou's nose, without baring his claws. Balou continued to pour kisses on Sunshine's face while still lying on her back. Sunshine took both of her front paws and began bouncing Balou's snout back and forth like he might do with a ball of string. Playful fighting ensued and soon Sunshine rolled on his back allowing Balou to push into his belly with her nose and tongue.

Sunshine's owner exited her back door

at the same time that Brian looked out of his back door. They both spied the two animals clawing and poking at each other like a brother and sister might play fight. Brian looked at the woman and shrugged, "I guess they each found a friend. Maybe Sunshine can come and visit Balou sometimes." The woman nodded in agreement.

The two animals had indeed each found a new friend.

Chapter 10

Big Sky - The Farm

During the winter, before the construction of the fence, Balou went on some long car rides to a place with wide open spaces and many different kinds of animals, including other dogs similar to her. Balou was allowed to take advantage of the warmth of the house at night, but was required to stay on a mat near the door whenever she was inside. In spite of the cold winter air, she enjoyed running outside all day with the other dogs, which were friendly and treated her well. They seemed to know so much more about this environment than she would ever know. This lack of knowledge was not a good thing for Balou.

Now that the winter was over and the chores around the city home, the yard and the fence, were complete, trips to this new place of wonder became more frequent. With the warmer summer weather, Balou was never invited inside the house, even at night. "Dogs are meant to be outside working, not inside lying about," the old woman who ran the house said.

The old man who seemed to be in charge of the outside world spent his days riding on big machines in the field and doing chores around the yard. The two boys from the family showed up twice each day to bring some large animals into a building and clamp collars around their necks, hook up some machines and work on the animals. Then the big plodding creatures were set free to roam in a field.

The farm dogs always followed the old man or the two boys in whatever activity they were performing. Balou was happy to follow along, but always seemed to get in the way and get scolded, while the other dogs were praised for their efforts. Each visit to the farm Balou learned more of the right things to do and less of the wrong things; her scoldings decreased and her praises increased. But she still made lots of mistakes – mistakes that cost her dearly.

When the boys wanted the big animals

to come to the barn, they made a strange sound from their mouths and the farm dogs ran out into the field where they chased the animals back to the building called a barn. Balou joined in and chased the big animals, delighting in watching them run away from her as she nipped at their heels.

"Balou, what do you think you're doing?" shouted one of the boys with an angry tone. "You're chasing them away. You're supposed to be bringing them in. Tramp, go get'em."

Tramp, the black and white dog raced after the escaping cow and forced it to turn around and head to the barn. Balou started to realize that they weren't supposed to just chase the animals, but chase them in a certain direction. Tramp was the leader of the farm dogs, all of whom followed her silent directions. Balou seemed to understand that it was in her interest to obey Tramp's lead.

One day Balou saw a lone young calf in the middle of a field and she decided to do the job she had been learning from Tramp. She ran as fast as she could after the calf, but the calf was too young to know it was supposed to run. As Balou approached the calf at full speed, the calf dropped his head to pull some grass from the ground, just as Balou smashed into the front of the calf's head. The calf jumped in surprise, but was barely touched by this forty-pound projectile. Balou, on the other hand, felt the full force of the crash and tumbled onto her back in the field as if she had been run down by a speeding car. Another lesson learned. If they don't run, stop chasing.

Balou continued to chase birds and rodents who all maintained established escape plans which kept Balou from even getting close to them. The big white birds in the yard were a different type of animal. They clucked and ran when Balou chased them, but she could catch them with little effort. This was fun as she grabbed one with her mouth, and squeezed it until it stopped moving. Then she moved to the next bird with the same results. Soon there were clumps of white feathers all over the yard. When the old man of the yard saw this, he exploded. He shouted and ran after Balou, kicking her in the side when he caught her. The force of the kick sent Balou rolling in the dirt with a pain in her side she had not felt since she was a puppy and had to visit the man in the white coat. The old man came at her with a big stick in his hand and

Balou ran for her life, experiencing a fear she had never known since the flashes of fire from the young men in her first home. She crawled under one of the buildings to escape the beating she knew was coming.

"Your darned dog killed half a dozen chickens," the old man shouted at Balou's masters. Brian retrieved Balou from her hiding place and although he didn't beat her, it was clear he was not happy. He took Balou around the yard and shouted at her as he pointed at the dead birds.

"We have to show her that she can never do this again," Brian said to Marlene as the tied one of the dead birds with a rope around Balou's neck. Balou was forced to spend the next day walking around with the dead bird dragging on the ground from her neck.

After this incident, she still liked to chase the farm birds, but she never touched them when she caught them. Every painful experience added to Balou's farm education.

Chapter 11

Black and White Cloud

Although the farm dogs treated Balou well, they were not much for playing and Balou liked to play. Tramp and the other dogs worked hard all day for the farmers, but when they weren't working, they rested and wouldn't budge. No amount of jumping, barking or nipping made these animals to move when it was rest time. They had learned to take full advantage of any time they didn't have to work, so they were rested and ready for their next chores.

It was during these rest periods that Balou wandered off by herself, to explore the wonders of the vast outdoor world that existed on the farm. She chased the wild birds, but they flapped away to the trees to escape her futile attack. She chased the little brown rodents, but they scurried into holes in the ground before she ever got near them. She tried digging after them, but couldn't make any progress in the hard clay that formed the homes for these little animals.

One day she spied a new quarry. It looked like some of the cats near her home who she had learned to be wary of because of their speedy sharp claws. This animal moved much slower than the cats. It waddled more than walked, but it had a long fluffy tail like a cat. It was all black with two white stripes down its back. Balou was sure she could catch this lumbering creature, but to avoid scaring it off as always happened with the birds and gophers, she decided to approach in silence.

Balou crouched low to the ground, edging forward only when the animal was not looking. Whenever the prey moved its head, Balou froze in one spot until the animal was not looking in her direction and then she sneaked forward a few more inches. The distance between Balou and the prey was now close enough that a quick pounce landed her on top of the animal before it knew what was happening.

Balou sprung for the black and white animal which showed no signs of fear as Balou began to descend on it. The animal didn't even turn to face her captor; it just raised its tail and Balou's world changed colour – a yellow mist sprayed into Balou's eyes, her face and her shoulders. Her eyes burned more than they ever had from the matches flashed in her face. Her whole head started to burn and she detected an odour like she had never experienced. She coughed and gagged from the stench that was now all over her body, turning her white fur to pale yellow. She dragged her front paws over her eyes and head, but that only worsened the pain. She tried rubbing her head on the ground, but again that didn't help. She saw the lumbering creature waddling off without any concern for Balou's predicament. Balou wanted to chase this devil and rip it to shreds, but she was too busy trying to rid herself of the foul poison that had engulfed her body.

After futile attempts at ridding herself of the scourge, Balou limped back to the farmyard to look for sympathy with her canine friends and her people. The farm dogs wouldn't come near Balou as she approached. They seemed to know what had happened and

81

ran from Balou as she neared them. She tried to chase after them, but she was too exhausted to try to keep up with their escape.

She lay whimpering outside the door to the house when Brian came out and saw her discoloured coat. He slammed the door shut before Balou could get close to the door and he stood on the inside looking at the forlorn animal.

"Marlene, get some tomato juice, Balou found a skunk," Brian called from behind the door.

Balou had to endure what seemed like hours of bathing in a red liquid while her masters coughed and gagged at the foul odour. Balou got no hugs or attention on the car ride home. She was relegated to the back seat with a wet blanket covering her body while her masters sat in the front seat uttering

what Balou understood to be very unkind
words directed at her.

She had learned another lesson. Next
time she would punish the devil who did this
to her.

Less than two weeks later Balou got her
chance. As she sat in the back seat of the car
to avoid the smoke from her masters, she
knew their destination was the farm. She
recognized the roads and buildings along the
now familiar route. As they got to the last

two miles of country roads, Balou began to prance in the back seat in anticipation of her revenge. She paced from window to window and whined with excitement.

"Settle down, Balou," called Brian from the driver's seat, "we're almost there.

Like a greyhound after a rabbit, Balou shot from the car when the door opened to let her out. After some brief play with the farm dogs that came to greet her she darted for the brush near the grassy field where she had last seen the monster that had defiled her. She sniffed the ground for a long time, along the edge of the field and into the wooded area. She could sense that her adversary had been here. She followed the scent that seemed to be getting fresher as she padded along the minute trails. After what seemed like an eternity of searching and following, she saw her prey. The black and white monster was lumbering along at a speed that was no match for Balou's. Balou assumed her stealth stand awaiting her chance to pounce and punish this cat-like monster. At what Balou thought was her best opportunity after creeping closer to the animal, she sprung at the beast. The result of her attack was all too familiar. The yellow spray burned her eyes and ears and soon the rest of her face and snout. She was delirious with the pain and foul odour that she couldn't rub off in the black dirt of the field. She lay in agony as her foe lumbered away, unfazed by the failed attack.

After Balou composed herself and built up enough resistance to her putrid smell, she limped back to the farmyard to accept her fate from her masters, who were again not very happy with Balou's adventures.

"She can just sit outside in her own stink," sneered Brian in disgust. "I'm not cleaning her up until we are ready to leave on Sunday."

Balou had a lonely and uncomfortable weekend, as no human would come near her and the farm dogs ran from her whenever she approached. The black and white monster had relegated her to an outcast and although she yearned for revenge against the beast, she now knew better than to attack this animal. But she would keep an eye on it if she saw it again.

Chapter 12

No Sunshine Here

Balou continued to make her treks to the home of the black and white monster, but stayed far away from the animal whenever she saw it. She just watched him waddle in the distance while she whined in both fear and excitement. Balou knew the fate that awaited her if she approached the beast, so she settled for just observation.

Balou noticed another slow moving animal that looked nothing like the beast with the yellow spray. This crawling quadruped looked more like the ball of wool her mistress used to make clothing. Easy prey, she thought as she crept up on the unsuspecting animal. Crouched with her belly scraping the ground, she saw her chance to attack with only inches separating her from her target. The pain from this encounter dwarfed the pain she felt from the black and white monster. As soon as she sprung upon the animal, it coiled into a ball and the soft wool that Balou was expecting turned into long hard nails that hammered their way into her mouth, her tongue, her lips and her nose. Balou pulled away in horror at the attack from this innocent looking creature that had just destroyed her face. She could not move her lips or her tongue and breathing through her nose was a near impossibility as her snout began to swell. Balou tried to push the long needles out of the way by dragging her face on the ground or against the trunk of a tree, but the more she tried, the deeper they lodged. She lay in defeat and agony watching the clumsy beast lumber away with apparent disinterest in Balou's incapacitated state.

It was early evening before Balou could assemble enough strength and determination to slink back to the farmyard to see if anyone took pity on her sad condition.

"Balou, where have you been?" Brian shouted as he saw Balou plod into view. "Marlene, pack some stuff, we have to get to the vet. Balou found a porcupine."

The car ride took Balou to a place she was familiar with and didn't like. She was placed on the metal table that allowed her no movement because she slipped every time she tried to move. She shivered as the man in the white coat approached her with an instrument that seemed to have a sharp end similar to those slivers sticking out of her face. That was Balou's last memory before waking up to find her face now clear of all the sharp pins, but instead with a throbbing pain that removed her desire to move.

After a couple of days of recovery, the ugly encounter was now a distant memory, but the thirst for revenge was even stronger than that for the black and white beast.

The next trip to the farm she sought her revenge and again the wild animal won out. Balou made another trip to the man with the white coat and metal table for repairs to her pin cushion face.

The farm, which had become such a place of fun and enjoyment, was also a place of great danger. Balou's education was progressing with every new lesson learned.

Chapter 13

Pot of Gold at the end of the Rainbow

Every trip to Brian's family's house was filled with excitement and agony in anticipation of seeing Snooky, the tiny white poodle that ruled this house. Balou tried with little success to befriend the yappy little runt. Sometimes she could get near enough to nuzzle the tiny animal, but often the encounter ended with Snooky yipping and taking a bite at the much larger dog. Balou never fought back against this little foe. Snooky spent most of her time sitting on the lap of the lady of the house and growling while Balou lay on the carpet with her sad eyes gazing at what she wanted to be her best friend.

Balou waged her tail as she chewed on a bone from the supper roast. Snooky watched with her mouth-watering. Balou, of course, was now a fifty-pound white German shepherd and Snooky was a four-pound poodle. No contest.

Snooky had no chance to pull the prize from the larger dog. It was time for an alternate approach. Snooky ran to the front door barking as if someone was coming to the door. Balou's curiosity showed immediately and she ran to the front door barking at the imaginary visitor. The bone sat alone in the middle of the floor. Snooky abandoned her position at the front door and ran to grab the bone and spirited it to the far corner of the room, her cropped tail wiggling in delight.

Balou realized that no one was coming to the door and returned to her position on the living room carpet, but the bone was gone. She looked over in to the corner and saw Snooky enjoying her winnings. Snooky coveted her prize and snarled as Balou gazed at the bone.

When Snooky abandoned the treasure to lap at some water in her nearby dish, Balou saw her opportunity to reclaim the bone without causing harm to her would-be friend. A quick pounce and once again Balou was chewing the bone, wagging her long white tail in satisfaction. Snooky was forced to look on, again drool dripping from her mouth in envy.

Snooky returned to her proven technique. She again ran to the front door barking at an imaginary visitor. Balou again started to run for the door. Half way to the front door Balou stopped in her tracks, turned back and picked up the bone. Balou managed a muffled bark at the non-existent visitor, with the bone held firmly in her teeth.

Snooky was smart, but Balou was a fast learner. More lessons for the young apprentice.

Chapter 14

Sunshine on the Water

Balou's masters began taking her on trips to a place that had a large expanse of water. This became one of her favourite outings and she could sense when she was getting close and jumped from the back seat to the front seat and back again, whining and panting in anticipation. She loved the freedom of roaming along the shore and barked at her masters or whoever else might be at hand to throw sticks into the water for her to swim out and retrieve. She could do this routine for hours and it seemed that her playmates, whether they were her owners, or someone else, tired of the game long before Balou did.

On one trip to a new place with water to swim in, she heard a noise in the next yard, some distance away. She looked over to see a little four-legged creature making a sound that resembled that of a loud bird. This animal was even smaller than Snooky, and only a bit larger than the brown rodents that burrowed into the ground only its spindly legs were longer. The sounds it made were directed at Balou. She could tell because this peaked-eared animal looked directly at Balou from the distance, baring its teeth as the shrill barking sounds flew from its tiny mouth.

Balou cocked her head with curiosity and after continued examination from her distant vantage point, she realized that this little animal was in fact another dog, just like her, only very tiny and without much hair. This was going to require some investigation.

The two yards were separated by a long ravine, filled with water. Balou knew that her masters did not approve of her drifting away from their sight, but she had to find out why this little yappy dog was calling to her. With her owners busy laughing and talking with the other people from the lake house, Balou began to saunter along the ravine looking for a way to cross over to the neighbouring yard to meet this little creature. The trip around the ravine was much longer than she expected, but she was able to navigate into the other yard where the yappy canine was directing its ire towards the big white intruder on its property. It stood its ground, yipping with all its might at Balou as she approached with caution. Balou got close enough to push her nose at the nose of the little one who stopped yapping long enough to sniff at Balou's snout. Balou was sure she had now tamed the wild beast and was ready to play and have fun.

The little one jumped back with a start at Balou's attempt to play and then lunged at Balou's face attempting to grab at whatever skin it could hold onto. Balou yelped in pain and jumped away. This tiny dog was not finished its assault on the much larger animal and again jumped at Balou, who backed away just in time. She turned her head in the opposite direction, tucked her tail between her legs and began to run from this vicious beast.

The people in the yard, who must be the masters of this wild animal, began to laugh as the spindly-legged aggressor began its pursuit of the fleeing giant. The little dog chased Balou around the ravine and into the yard where Balou was running to seek the protection of her masters. But they didn't protect her, they just laughed as the little animal continued to chase and attack Balou. "Balou, you coward," Brian shouted as Balou ran by with the tiny animal, this size of an overgrown gopher, chasing after the terrified white German Shepard, "that's a Chihuahua your running from, you could eat it with one bite."

The larger animal was finally able to put enough distance between her had the tiny devil that she felt in no further danger. She waited until the smaller dog had returned to its yard before slinking back to her masters who offered no sympathy, only ridicule and laughter.

Balou was not a fighter and wasn't prepared to hurt this vicious animal any more than she could cause harm to her nemesis, Snooky. Balou felt no need for revenge against these animals who humiliated her as she had for the wild animals at the farm.

Chapter 15

Who's New Under the Sun

Balou got used to the ever changing environment in her home. The basement started to grow walls and soft flooring. The yard was now enclosed and there was grass and other vegetation growing on the previously dirt and mud surface. The windows in the house became covered in fabric and new furniture appeared in every room.

So when other items started appearing, Balou gave them no thought. A tiny bed in one of the bedrooms and a basket on wheels meant nothing to Balou. The basket made a comfortable place to lie under as it provided what felt like a roof over her head. The increasing size of her mistress was nothing that attracted her attention. Balou still got her regular trips to the farm and to the house where Snooky lived. She received lots of love and attention and was never lacking for water or food. In fact she found a way to get treats on demand just by moving her body in certain ways. If she sat on her haunches and held her front paws limp in front of her, she received a biscuit or a crust of sandwich. Standing on her hind legs resulted in even more treats. The simple act of rolling on the floor caused her master to toss her some goodies.

One day the farmer and his wife showed up at the house and took Balou to the farm with them. This was the first time she had ever made the trip without her masters, but the farm was the farm even if her masters weren't there; she loved the farm life – as long as she avoided the creatures that attacked her.

After a few days of playing on the farm, the farmers again loaded her in the truck and brought her back to her home. She wagged her tail and jumped up on her masters to show how happy she was to see them again. The farmers were fine people, but they never gave her any special attention like her masters did.

While the farmers and her masters sat in the big room and talked, Balou nestled herself under the basket on wheels to have a deep sleep to rest up after her time spent running around the farm. She had no idea how long she had been in her sound sleep when she almost jumped to the ceiling with fright from a screech she had never heard in her life. The basket on wheels began to vibrate and rock and screeching noises spilled from within, while the people in the room began laughing at Balou and her surprised antics. Once she had overcome her fear of the movement and the screeching noise, she stood on her hind legs to peer into the basket to see what was causing the basket to move and come alive. As she gazed inside the basket, she saw a small bundle of cloth with a tiny human face contorted and screaming.

"Looks like Balou has discovered Tony," Brian said to the others in the room. Marlene walked over to the basket and picked up the little living creature and showed it to Balou who was both fearful and curious. She wanted to push her nose at the creature, but as she got close, more noise emanated from the face of the creature and scared her away. Everyone in the room laughed at Balou's response.

Marlene held and rocked the little human and placed him on the sofa still wrapped in blankets. Balou walked up to the baby, sniffed him and then sat on her haunches at attention, with the baby at her back while she peered outward towards whatever or whoever might approach the new member of the house. Something deep inside Balou began to play with her mind. She knew this was an important day and this was an important creature. She knew she could never allow anyone near this tiny animal without her blessings. Only those with the best intentions for the baby were ever allowed near. Balou had a new mission in life.

Balou lay near the basket or the tiny bed whenever Tony was resting; watching to make sure everything was OK. When Tony stirred, Balou ran to Marlene and coax her to drop whatever she was doing and come to the aid of the little life that now became the centre of her masters' attention.

Balou was now banned from the bed she shared with her masters and had to sleep on the floor beside them. "I need my rest," Marlene complained to Brian who made sure that Balou didn't sneak up onto the mattress during the night. Balou missed sleeping between the two warm bodies and she attributed this new arrangement to the arrival of the newcomer to the house. But she never resented Tony for her altered sleeping arrangement. Tony was her responsibility and she took that role seriously.

Before long, Tony was moving on his belly on the carpet trying to grab at Balou. Balou never complained whenever Tony reached her and grab at her ears or tail, or poke at her eyes. She tried to avoid having Tony molest her by moving away, but when Tony was too quick, she just accepted her fate.

Creeping on the carpet turned to crawling and then to walking. Tony was getting faster in his movement around the house. This created two problems for Balou. The first was that there were more dangers that she had to protect Tony from and the second was that there was more chance that Tony reached Balou and pull at her body parts or hair.

Still she just accepted the friendly abuse as part of her role as Tony's protector.

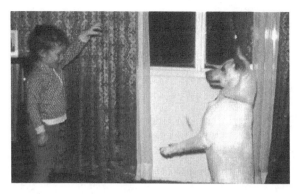

One day she was again pulled away from the house by the farmers for a trip to the farm without her family. When she returned a few days later, she saw a familiar routine emerge. The previously still basket on wheels began to move and sounds emanated from it. Standing on her hind legs as she had two years earlier, she spied another little life in the basket.

"Balou, meet Cameron, Tony's new little brother," Brian said as he held the new addition to the family for Balou to inspect. Balou's role became more complex as she now had two tiny humans to care for and two little boys who both wanted to pull at her ears and poke her eyes. But she didn't mind; they were her family.

Soon Cameron began to creep, then crawl, then walk. Balou followed the two boys everywhere when they were outside playing. She knew the dangers of the outside world and made sure that none of those dangers affected her boys.

Chapter 16

Sand Castles in the Sun

When the family went to the lake, Balou sensed it wasn't a good idea for either of the boys to approach the water without one of her big masters along with them. Balou knew how to chase a stick thrown into the water, but she doubted the boys would fare as well if they chased into the water after an object, such as the balls they liked to toss around. Balou loved to chase the ball when the boys threw it or kicked it. If it was a small ball, she grabbed it in her mouth and brought it back to one of the boys who threw it again for her to chase. If it was one of the bigger balls that they kicked, she pushed it with her nose to retrieve it for the boys.

If one of the boys began venturing in the direction of the dangerous water, Balou forgot about the ball and ran after either Tony or Cam and as gently as she could, she bumped them to the ground and bark until one of the masters came to investigate. She knew they shouldn't be near the water alone.

Lying on the warm sand near the water with her eyes fluttering in near sleep was one of Balou's favourite relaxing activities. She kept one eye half open all the time, just to see where the two boys were playing, making sure she could come to their aid if needed. While nearly dozing in the sand, the boys often started tossing handfuls of sand on Balou's body.

In short order, she found that the only part of her body that wasn't completely covered in sand was her head; she was buried up to her neck with only her head visible above the sand which was almost the same colour as she, making her nearly invisible on the beach. As long as the boys stayed nearby, Balou relished this activity, giving her a sense of physical security. However if the boys strayed too far and looked like they might need her, she pushed with all her might to remove the sand from on top of her and chase after the boys.

Chapter 17

Winter Sunshine

"Look what I got you, Balou," Brian spoke with excited words as he held out an apparatus that Balou didn't recognize. It didn't look like a toy, and it didn't look like food. It was more like the strap that sometimes Brian attached to Balou to keep her from running loose. Brian fit the straps over Balou's head and under her belly, while she stood still, sensing that she wasn't supposed to fight back or play. "There, perfect fit," Brian exclaimed, as Balou just stood and stared at Brian.

Balou bounced with excitement when Brian reached for his heavy coat as this was the signal for a trip outside into the yard which was covered in deep white powder that Balou like to romp in. The apparatus around her shouldn't restrict her playing in the snow.

"They're ready," Marlene said as she delivered the two boys dressed up so tight in heavy clothing that they waddled when they walked. It looked like Balou was going to have some company to play with in the yard.

When they exited the front door, there stood a wood and metal toy that Balou had seen her masters use to pull the boys on some of their winter walks. Brian sat both boys in their heavy snowsuits on the sled and then hooked a leash to the straps around Balou.

"OK, Balou, let's go," Brian called as he ran forward. Balou tried to obey but when she had only taken a few steps she skidded to a halt as she found she was attached to the sled that carried the two boys. Brian kept calling to Balou, but she just stood there wondering how she was to come when she was anchored by this big toy.

"Maybe it's too heavy with the two of them," Brian called to Marlene who was watching from the doorway. "Tony, here you get off and we'll try it with just Cam." Brian lifted Tony from the sled and stood him on the cleared sidewalk and again called to Balou. She started to walk towards him, but was again restrained by the sled.

"Here, let me give you a hand," Brian said as he grabbed the strap connecting the sled to Balou and gave it a tug. "Now, go Balou," he said. Balou just looked around at him. Where was she to go?

"OK, let's try this. Tony, you go out in front of Balou and I'll push the sled while you call her. Tony obeyed his dad and waddled a short distance in front of Balou and gave a muffled call through his covered face, "Here, Boo." Balou could feel the strap slacken as Brian pushed the sled, so she obeyed Tony and started walking towards him. After several steps, the strap went taught and Balou stopped at the weight of the sled with Cam aboard.

"Cam, here you get out too and we'll see if Balou can do it empty," Brian said and he lifted the younger boy out of the sled and set him on the ground beside. "Now Balou, come," Brian said running out in front of Balou. She started to walk and realized she had enough power to move the empty contraption, so she followed Brian as he walked ahead leaving the boys standing in the snow. "There, good girl. OK Cam get in and let's go," Brian shouted with excitement. As soon as Cam sat down on the sled, the weight again caused Balou to stop in the snow.

This activity continued as Brian tried everything to get Balou to pull the sled with one or both boys in it. But nothing worked. Balou got confused with what this activity was supposed to do. She just wanted to run in the snow.

"I guess she's just not cut out to be a sled dog," Brian conceded to Marlene who was still watching from the doorway for some evidence of progress. Brian tried for two days to get Balou to pull the sled, but in the end, he hung the harness on a hook near the door and Balou never wore it again.

Chapter 18

The Sun Rises

As the two boys grew larger, Balou had to spend more time at the house alone. It seemed that her masters were always taking the boys out somewhere and leaving her behind. In the summer weather, sometimes Balou was brought along, but kept on a leash that restricted her from going too far. She lay in the grass watching her boys run in the fields with many other children, chasing a ball. She sometimes whined and tried to pull free from the chain that constrained her so she too could chase the ball with the children. But that wasn't allowed; this seemed to be some organized activity that none but the children could participate in – not even the big people, like her masters.

In the winter, the boys packed bags into the car and Balou was taken to the farm while her masters and the boys left on frequent trips.

As Balou spent more and more of her time at the farm, she missed the days when she could come into the house from the cold wind and snow. But she found that her white coat became thicker, protecting her from the worst of the weather. There were lots of warm places to curl up and rest to keep out of the bitter winds. The barn, the haystacks, the piles of baled straw, near the cattle, or sometimes even inside the little house for the white birds.

The trips back to her home in the city became more infrequent. Her masters, especially the man, came to see her at the farm and play with her, giving her attention, but he always had to leave. Soon the trips to the house in the city ceased altogether and the farm became her full-time home. She still saw her masters and her boys, who were getting very big, but they had little time for her. She missed them all, but she was happy and content with her life at the farm. There was always a lot to do, she had her freedom, and she was never hungry as the lady farmer always tossed out food from the house that Balou and the other dogs shared.

Balou and the other dogs especially liked the big bones that the lady tossed out to them. Life on the farm was about survival, both for the animals and for the humans who ran the farm. Survival of the humans appeared to be the most important thing from what Balou could tell. She sensed that the bones on which she gnawed came from the big animals in the field that sometimes disappeared. This made her twinge knowing that animals existed only to satisfy the needs of the humans.

Tramp was never much of a playmate for Balou, and Balou saw that he was moving slower. There were new younger dogs that had appeared and they loved to run with Balou, but Tramp just lay around the yard, not even chasing the big animals anymore. He sometimes struggled to try to fetch the cattle twice daily, but his tired old legs would not carry him like they used to. Balou awoke one morning and didn't see Tramp among the other dogs. Balou had not seen Tramp since the previous evening when the farmer took him for a walk in the field. Tramp could no longer perform the chores required of the dogs for survival on the farm. Tramp never returned from his walk.

Chapter 19

The Sun Also Sets

Although Balou missed her family, as she saw them infrequently, she loved her life on the farm. She had freedom of movement, lots of food and water; but she lacked the attention she had grown to love. Nights in the warm soft bed with two bodies beside her, were just a distant, but pleasant memory. She had long ago ceased begging to enter the farm house.

Summer followed winter, winter followed summer in a continuous rhythm. Balou began to move slower, not able to keep up with the younger dogs anymore when they chased the cows. Her legs and back hurt when she moved. Balou found herself lying in the hay more often than she ever used to. It was comfortable to curl up and rest rather than putting in the effort to run with the young farm dogs. One day she curled up in a ball as usual to protect against the wind and snow. The warmth from the hay around her made her body relax. She closed her eyes and dreamed. She dreamed of the times that had passed – her first masters, who were kind and cruel at the same time; her new doting masters and the home they provided; her first trips to the farm; the trips to the lake; the encounters with Snooky; and so much more. The dreaming stopped and Balou fell into a deep sleep and she was content.

"What will we tell Brian? Balou was always his pet," asked the old farmer of his wife as the two of them found Balou curled up in the hay.

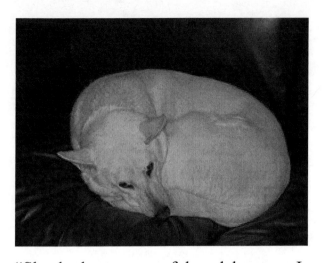

"She looks so peaceful and happy. I think she is smiling," responded the old woman. "I'll tell him she passed away with a smile on her face. She had a good life, and a long life. Balou made it past thirteen years, you know. That's old for a dog. She left this world on her own terms."

###

You may contact the author at:

brianborgford@outlook.com

Read other stories by Brian Borgford at

Amazon.com.

Made in the USA
Middletown, DE
14 April 2017